Rookie
Read-About® Holidays

Groundhog Day

By Michelle Aki Becker

Consultant
Don L. Curry
Reading and Content Consultant

Children's Press ®
A Division of Scholastic Inc.
New York   Toronto   London   Auckland   Sydney
Mexico City   New Delhi   Hong Kong
Danbury, Connecticut

Designer: Herman Adler Design
Photo Researcher: Caroline Anderson
The photo on the cover shows a groundhog eating clover.

Library of Congress Cataloging-in-Publication Data

Becker, Michelle Aki.
  Groundhog Day / by Michelle Aki Becker ; Don Curry, reading and
content consultant.
        p. cm. – (Rookie read-about holidays)
Summary: Introduces the history of Groundhog Day and explains how it is
observed today.
Includes index.
  ISBN 0-516-25883-4 (lib. bdg.)   0-516-27924-6 (pbk.)
  1. Groundhog Day–Juvenile literature. [1. Groundhog Day. 2.
Holidays.] I. Title. II. Series.
  GT4995.G76B43 2003
  394.261–dc21
                                2003000461

CHILDREN'S PRESS, and ROOKIE READ-ABOUT®,
and associated logos are trademarks and or registered trademarks
of Scholastic Library Publishing. SCHOLASTIC and associated logos
are trademarks and or registered trademarks of Scholastic Inc.
  4 5 6 7 8 9 10 R 12 11 10 09 08 07

Will the groundhog see his shadow this year?

People all over the country celebrate (SEL-uh-brate) Groundhog Day on February 2.

February 2006

Sunday	Monday	Tuesday	Wednesday	Thursday	Friday	Saturday
			1	2	3	4
5	6	7	8	9	10	11
12	13	14	15	16	17	18
19	20	21	22	23	24	25
26	27	28				

Groundhog Day takes place near the end of winter.

When will winter end?
When will spring begin?
On Groundhog Day, you
might find out the answers.

Groundhogs are small, furry animals. They are also called woodchucks (WUD-chuhks).

Groundhogs live in burrows.
Burrows are tunnels they dig
in the ground. They rest in
the burrows all winter and
come out in the spring.

In the little town of Punxsutawney (PUNKS-sa-taw-nee), Pennsylvania, there is one special groundhog.

His name is Punxsutawney Phil.

Can Phil tell if there will be
six more weeks of winter?

On Groundhog Day, people come to Gobbler's (GAHB-lurz) Hill. They wait for Phil to come out of a hole.

Will Phil see his shadow?

If it is sunny, there will be a shadow. People say that if Phil sees his shadow, winter will last for another six weeks.

If it is cloudy, there will not
be a shadow. People say if
Phil does not see his shadow,
spring will come early.

Sometimes the groundhog
is right. Sometimes he
is wrong.

People still celebrate
Groundhog Day because
it is fun.

18

People started celebrating this day in Europe (YU-ruhp) in the 1600s.

In Europe they used hedgehogs (HEJ-hogs) to tell what the weather would be.

Groundhog Day was started in 1887 by an editor and a congressman (KONG-griss-man) in Pennsylvania.

The little town of Punxsutawney became known as the "Weather Capital of the World."

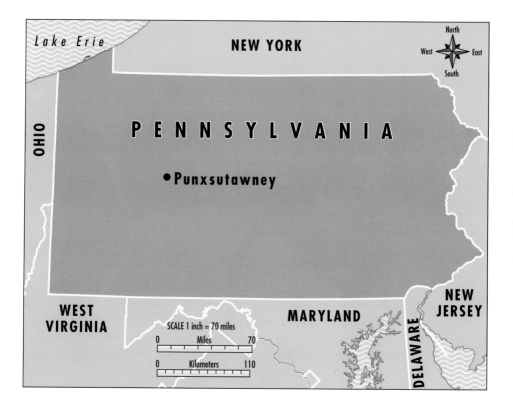

Phil is on the news the day of the celebration.

Everyone in the country can see him.

Hundreds of people now come to Punxsutawney to celebrate Groundhog Day.

Phil lives in a special home
with two other groundhogs.
It is in the Punxsutawney
public library.

Groundhog Day is fun!

Will Punxsutawney Phil predict when spring will come this year?

Words You Know

Gobbler's Hill

groundhog

hedgehog

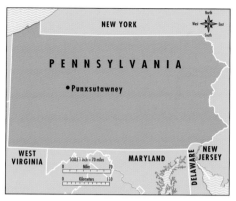

Punxsutawney

shadow

spring

winter

31

Index

About the Author

Michelle Aki Becker lives in New York City. She has written a number of nonfiction children's books.

Photo Credits

Photographs © 2003: Alan Freed/Punxsutawneyphil.com: 24, 27; AP/Wide World Photos/Gene J. Puskar: 12, 13, 29, 30 top; Corbis Images: 20 (Bettmann), 3, 30 bottom left (John Conrad), 26 (David Maxwell/AFP); Peter Arnold, Inc/Fred Bruemmer: 8; Photo Researchers, NY/Anne Fournier: 9; PhotoEdit/ Spencer Grant: 7, 31 bottom left; The Image Works/Peter Hvizdak: 17; Visuals Unlimited: cover, 18, 30 bottom right (Joe McDonald), 6, 31 bottom right (Jim Whitmer).

Illustrations by Paul Rowntree

Maps by Bob Italiano